POETRY BY BARBARA HOWES

Looking Up at Leaves   1966

Light and Dark   1959

In the Cold Country   1954

The Undersea Farmer   1948

EDITED BY BARBARA HOWES

From the Green Antilles:
  WRITINGS OF THE CARIBBEAN   1966

23 Modern Stories   1963

LOOKING UP AT LEAVES

BARBARA HOWES

LOOKING UP AT LEAVES

 NEW YORK · ALFRED · A · KNOPF · 1966

*Certain of these poems appeared
in the following periodicals and anthologies:*

The Atlantic; Berkshire Review; Bim (*Barbados*); The
Carleton Miscellany; Encounter (*England*); The Massachusetts
Review; The New Republic; The New York Times; Redbook;
Saturday Review; The Southern Review; Stand (*England*); The
Virginia Quarterly Review; Modern American Poetry *edited by Louis
Untermeyer*; Of Poetry and Power *edited by Erwin Glikes and
Paul Schwaber*; The Golden Journey *edited by Louise Bogan and
William Jay Smith*; Isak Dinesen: A Memorial *edited by Clara
Svendsen*; Under Månens Skive *edited by Elsa Gress* (*Denmark*).

The poems "A Letter from the Caribbean," "On Galveston Beach,"
"Flight," "Sea School," "The Bay at West Falmouth," and "Ode
to Poseidon" appeared originally in *The New Yorker*.

The poems "Troy Weight Taken," "A Conversation," "Thinking
of K.H.S.," "The Crane Chub—Barbados," "At the Blue Mill
Tavern," "What Bird," "Dream of a Good Day," "A Stand of
Birches," "Footnote," "The Cisisbeae," "Town Meeting Tuesday,"
"Radar and Unmarked Cars," "The Lonely Box," "Headlong,"
"On Falling Asleep in a Mountain Cabin," and "The Dressmaker's
Dummy as Scarecrow" appeared originally in *Poetry*.

This is a Borzoi Book published by Alfred A. Knopf, Inc.

First Edition

© *Copyright 1959, 1961, 1962, 1963, 1964, 1965, 1966 by Barbara Howes
All rights reserved under International and Pan-American Copyright Conventions.
Distributed by Random House, Inc. Published simultaneously in Toronto,
Canada, by Random House of Canada Limited.
Library of Congress Catalog Card Number: 66–19381
Manufactured in the United States of America*

Harriott Allen

There was always this groundswell of love—
Now—a wave on the beach—it is all over:
There is no message left upon the sand.
Mother-of-pearl worn hollow, I bend
To listen for that greygreen groundswell.

CONTENTS

FOR

Charlee and Dick Wilbur

PART I

A Short Way by Air

Out Fishing

We went out, early one morning,
Over the loud marches of the sea,
In our walnut-shell boat,
Tip-tilting over that blue vacancy.

Combering, coming in,
The waves shellacked us, left us breathless, ill;
Hour on hour, out
Of this emptiness no fish rose, until

The great one struck that twine-
Wrapped flying-fish hard, turned and bolted
Off through the swelling sea
By a twist of his shoulder, with me tied fast; my rod

Held him, his hook held me,
In tug-of-war—sidesaddle on the ocean
I rode out the flaring waves,
Rode till the great fish sounded; by his submersion

He snapped the line, we lost
All contact; north, south, west, my adversary
Storms on through his world
Of water: I do not know him: he does not know me.

Dead Toucan: Guadeloupe

Down like the oval fall of a hammer
The great bill went,
Trailed by its feather-duster body
Splat on cement.
His mates fell out of countenance,
All listened, shivering in the sun,
For what was off, amiss:
In his pretend haven under a flame tree
The agouti crouched, chewed on his spittle, shook,
The porcupine rolled in his box, the parakeets
Chattered regrets,
Knowing something was wrong in their hot Eden:
That their King had followed his heavy fate to earth;
And his superb
Accomplishment,
His miracle of balance,
Had come to nothing, nothing. . . .
A beak with a panache
Chucked like an old shell back to the Caribbean.

Troy Weight Taken

We do not need to comb
Arkansas to find
Rubies; loneliness
Vanishes in this crystal-
Clear actual air,
And one by one makes one.
Love tempers us, and every
True embrace is carved
In ivory, lasts; although
My eyes are shut, I learn
Each golden day that golden
Moorings hold me home.

A Letter from the Caribbean

Breezeways in the tropics winnow the air,
Are ajar to its least breath
But hold back, in a feint of architecture,
The boisterous sun
Pouring down upon

The island like a cloudburst. They
Slant to loft air, they curve, they screen
The wind's wild gaiety
Which tosses palm
Branches about like a marshal's plumes.

Within this filtered, latticed
World, where spools of shadow
Form, lift and change,
The triumph of incoming air
Is that it is there,

Cooling and salving us. Louvers,
Trellises, vines—music also—
Shape the arboreal wind, make skeins
Of it, and a maze
To catch shade. The days

Are all variety, blowing;
Aswirl in a perpetual current
Of wind, shadow, sun,
I marvel at the capacity
Of memory

Which, in some deep pocket
Of my mind, preserves you whole—
As wind is wind, as the lion-taming
Sun is sun, you are, you stay:
Nothing is lost, nothing has blown away.

A Conversation

FOR ISAK DINESEN

As we stood on the crushed stone
Of the drive, it was as if
A spring landscape unrolled
Between. Colors deep
As gems—the tapestry,
Intricate and rich,
Of a lifetime. I was
Assumed into this world;
These emblematic hues
Shone like vintage wine:
Jet—that contains darkness
For those who have known the worst;
Beige—parchment-colored,
On which a burning glass
Etches the mind's runes;
Turquoise—that mood of green
And blue, field and sky—
Blending, to stand out.
Artist and woman moved there
Each in her separate light,
Clear-cut against a silver
Background of dream—all
Colors blend in silver,
A molten gong—whose full
Resonance an artist
Brocades upon the soul.

On Galveston Beach

The sky was battened down
Low all around us. We stood up
Into a sea of air,
First comers to this Sicilian element,
Prospectors motionless in a bowl of blue.

Down-at-mouth at the rim,
The barely-breathing sea
Neighbored flat sand; it waited
As a pier does for some sightseer
Of horizons to wander out.

If the sky is indeed a bowl
Pressed over us by a huge hand,
We have fellow-creatures everywhere:
Sand in its patient minuteness,
That lean duck, his neck a hook, bobbing for fish,
Or those great mushrooms of the Gulf,
Jetsam jellyfish, in whose gills
Lie strands of aquamarine;
Their lives, so humpbacked and so white,
Resemble death. We stand awhile and watch
Waves worry them toward shore,
Before striking out in their sea.

Flight

One bails out into space
Each morning, distance

Is nothing: a subway stop,
A walk uphill. The Russian, well-equipped,

Trod space as though man had been twirling there
Always, a bauble on the chandelier

Of the firmament; attached by a beanie
Headdress, Leonov was fully

Aware that should the cord break
It would take

No time for him to die: or go
On into limbo,

A man-made satellite. . . . But he was
Under the proud eye of the world, unlike Goya's

Madman circling Toledo
Like a Barnum and Bailey missile

With no intent
Of destruction, lent

Terror only from his own terror,
Who rode the air

Hellbent, though no one thought to look up. . . .
A boy stepped

Into one car
Not the next, one segment of the river

Of the subway, and entered upon his death
As much by chance as by the icepick in his brain, the wealth

Of his unlived good years
Spent in a moment; all our fear

Of the unknown, revulsion at brutality
Casts us out to the outer spaces of the mind, whence we

Will return only with time,
Realizing of him

That nothing is the same as one young man, one son,
One good bet, gone.

On Sleeping Together

Day becomes explicit. From this shared
Warmth we grew into together here in bed,
Concave as a hammock, we are all one piece
At the moment of waking: is that my arm, or this?
Still linked and folded, slowly we withdraw
Selves and bodies from our world of sleep.
Caught in silhouette, heroic figures
Dim in the toils of darkness, but now responding
To the bravura of conch-shell and drum,
Alive, we wake; waking, we separate,
With ceremony rise to greet the morning.

For Chloe

My cat kneads me with her rhythmic paws,
But this is in reverie, a work of affection;
She may see this warm base as a high table
Near which, below the salt, her mouse is et,
She wants thereafter her dark glade of purring,
And a breathing body under her ribcase.

For Cleo

A different nature wanders through the door,
Brushing each corner in her satisfaction,
Curving by man, by furniture, well able
As any golden cat to charm and wait
Her golden due; she is; she warms a long slurring
Breath of congratulation, being at ease.

A Near-Pantoum for a Birthday

At my Grandmother's life I look,
In this my fiftieth year of age,
Not a recluse, like her, not dark,
Withdrawn; for love is my stage.

In this my fiftieth year of age,
I'll figure out my place, and not
Withdraw, for love is my stage;
Loving and loved in this green spot,

I'll single out my place, not
As she the suburb of despair
(Loving and loved in this green spot)
Who breathed the shadows of the air.

As she—the suburbs of despair,
The cold body, the cold heart,
Who breathed the shadows of the air,
Denying love, kept all apart.

The cold body, the cold heart!
May this next decade see my warmth
Preserving love in every part;
Let me be held in my love's arms!

May these next years contain my warmth—
At Grandmother's thin life I look—
Let me hold love, then, in my arms,
Not a recluse, all quick, not dark.

The Lace Maker

Needle, needle, open up
The convolvulus of your eye,
I must come upon it quick
Or my thread will die.

Night is settling down outside,
My sallow candle seems to thin,
But I must weave this laddered thread
To nest each rare space in.

It is dark. Darkness plaits a scarf
Over my eyes. Can finger sprout
Eyes at the tip to guide its work?
Each evening, I go out

To Sainte Gudule—if I can see
Needlepoint of aspiring stone,
The window's rose embroidery
Trained like a trumpet upon Heaven,

Then I may live; but if my sight
Narrows toward death, a black-avised
Gargoyle will jut out, grinning there,
Exulting in that swirling mist.

The Crane Chub—Barbados

Darling,
I learn
The full
Value
Of you
Again,
Savoring
The Crane
Chub
Who idles,
Mates,
And dies,
Near one
Single
Reef
Just off
St. Philip
Parish;
He loves
His own,
Is of
A flesh
So rare
He must
Be eaten
Just
Within
The hour.

As your
Absence
Goes so
Against
The tide—
Sun,
Love,
Wind—
I now
Partake
Of Crane
Chub:
And oh
His essence
Is
Less rare,
Bitter,
Within
The flaw
Of your
Not being
Here.

Thinking of K.H.S.

All loss brings us to character.
Real loss implies some dear
Distinct mind and figure; thus to recall
Nervous, kind, clear

Vignettes is as important as it is moving.
But when we should have begun
To see life standing with death white at its shoulder
And have realized that this living

Woman should have been welcomed face
To face, I cannot now
Say. Our lives were rivercraft which turned
Up different streams to lose

Touch. Then in my humdrum health
I looked toward old affection:
Only to be brought up short by the unyielding
Grey sentence of your death.

On a Statue by Lehmbruck

FOR MY GODCHILD

In this cold chambered light
The young body is cool
As stoneware; beneath the dome's
Chill parasol of glass she kneels,
Suppliant as a vase.

The body is a vase: each orifice
Breathes between two worlds,
As, in its innocence, a bay window,
That belled membrane of glass,
Holds off the weather and conducts light.

Compliant, on one knee, withdrawn
And bare the statue waits
Till it will rise a woman, and will know
What winds blow through the storm-house of the body,
To penetrate or fill.

Beautiful and single, a vase still,
Turn, now turn your clear eye, true as glass,
Toward the future. May you come to bear
The full body of love
Not its stigmata.

19

The Lovers of Delicate Things

IN MEMORIAM: WPD

William and I
    Always want too much—
Want people to be porcelain
    But also willing;
Want the sensitive brain
    To triumph over the doings

Of the rough outside world.
    William and I
Seem to be obdurate, only
    We melt at the ring
Of the wrong number, at the
    Wild hope that everything

Is about to work
    Out according to our notions.
William and I
    Balk, check rein
On the stampede of those ponies
    Within us, strike out from our pain

With sharp hooves.
    It is better to be lonely
Than wrong, we think, or tasteless.
    William and I,
By giving up, give less
    Of ourselves to be hurt. By

Self-effacement, that Puritan
    Mask, do we conceal
The structure of our pride.
    We should have turned,
William and I,
    Away from power, have learned

That control is not needed
    Over others; simply of oneself, for
The lover of delicate things
    Can reach out and destroy
That to which he most clings—
    William!—Not I!

Gulls

In their long
Arabesque, wings ferrying the steady
Cargo of the body,
Are strong

As mainsails;
Yet cutting into the sky they cut out paper–
Birds: themselves, shape;
They sickle

All that's in view,
Outrunning the westering tide in the face of the west
Wind, across distance—
ᗰ to ധ — ᗰ to ധ .

At the Blue Mill Tavern

So lucid was that night,
The stars in their great chandelier
Ranged low above our heads.
   Arrayed for evening, we
   Continued on till neon script
   Coralled us; we went in,

To find our corner table, ordering
Sociably, elbow to elbow. . . . Spaced
Like piano-keys along the bar,
The pretzel-eaters hunched,
Their bivouac a beer.
   Time on its pendulum
   Swung loosely, as when love
   Puts out the clock.

Talking around
Another round, the walls
Began to tilt; we teetered above the wet
Rings on the table. Affection
Fled far out like pastel wind-
Sleeves at an airport. Holding
   Hands, lost to each other's
   Thought, we nodded: the bartender
   Set glasses on a tray.

Suddenly we were caught
Up in a windmill's savage arms,
Whirled blue in that wash of air;
Insatiable, like gulls, we swayed
Crying havoc over this charivari,
This tinsel world.
    An ill wind: the clocks have blown apart;
    Falling, falling where memory cannot follow,
    The mist received us, and we were not there.

Footnote

Love is a great leveler.
Some of us
May fancy we have mastered desire—
Not likely; it's too imperious. For many
Love is a great
Barrier; some are ill
With fear of it. Few, really,
Have ever breathed its blue oracular air
Deep in their lungs. Love is a bell
That sounds and bodies forth the whole being.
We need own
So little: half a bed;
So much: hope that love is, will be
Love.

A Stand of Birches

FOR R.W.

Tall as if standing on jointed stilts,
This upright scaffolding,
These delicate laths
Firm to an altitude,
Much as 7-league boots might change
The gangling third son of all fairy-tale
To one fit to win The Princess.

There is something in this silhouette
Of courtier and hobbledehoy,
Opposites strung like wire over the high
Paneling of the shoulders: impatient, cool;
A laconic herald;
Pan in an Ascot tie.

There is a gardener, too, stubborn, yare,
Whose work terraces the hillsides
Of language, possessed
By a nomad cast of mind that ranges
Furlongs over a landscape
Of solitude and distance.

Something that Holbein would have paused
Over informs this face:
He might have seen—
Painted on wood—the clean
Jaw and square brow, caught in those shadowed eyes
Vision that brought cathedrals higher, higher,
Lofty as there was stone for them;
All lit, all colored by
A heaviness of light,
New England Gothic chiaroscuro.

So, like a stand of birches, be briary, bend,
Touch earth, whip back to your high stance again.

Dream of a Good Day

I dream of going in my outrigger canoe—
Buoyant, in balance upon each cobalt wave—
To follow the porpoise at his crescent play.

Or in my schooner, at its easy riding,
To imagine high in the crow's-nest—which the ship
Sedately nods this way and that—a bed
Of crimson peonies, mine for the conceiving.

After, to wander alone the high wind-lanes,
With language all one's passion: its topsail
Scudding—then made fast: the poem strengthening,
Quieting down. . . . A day to dream of—
Then in the colloquial evening to come back to love.

What Bird

What bird was that, in the corner,
The cat brought in? I resurrect
No more than this scatter of dark
Plumage, household graffiti
To add to the lore of the dump.
Colorless, bodiless, less the bird
That inhabited this costume
And which proved its former mastery
Of air, by failing that once;—
Like anyone else who does badly
Sometimes: feathers in the corner: a dunce.

Sea School

This afternoon I swam with a school of fish.
Waiting in shallow water for the tide to change,
They swept at leisure through their green pleasance
Turning at will as one, or at some private
Signal all felt:
White and delicate, each one bedizened
By an ochre spot behind his sickle of gill,
Pale translucent fish they were, divided
By the hair-thin moustache-line of backbone.

We plied our way along, taking our ease,
In concert, as a school
Feeling the flickering lozenges of light,
Chickenwire of sunlight grazing us
As we passed up and down under its stroke.
So for an hour, an age, I swam with them,
One with the rhythm of the sea, weightless,
Graceful and casual in our schoolhood,
Within our coop of light,
One with a peace that might go on forever. . . .
Till, of a sudden, quick as a falling net,
Some thought embraced them: I watched them go
Tidily over the reef where I could not follow.

The Bay at West Falmouth

Serenity of mind poises
Like a gull swinging in air,
At ease, sculptured, held there
For a moment so long-drawn-out all time pauses.

The heart's serenity is like the gold
Geometry of sunlight: motion shafting
Down through green dimensions, rung below rung
Of incandescence, out of which grace unfolds.

Watching that wind schooling the bay, the helterskelter
Of trees juggling air, waves signalling the sun
To signal light, brings peace: as our being open
To love does, by this serenity of water.

My Dear, Listen:

If what may be
Is to turn—by grace, by craft, into poetry,
Is it not fine
That there are ten
Or more varieties
Of wild cherry,
And as for maples
There are multiple
Sorts that range
All over our ancient
American topsoil?
But then all
Of these fair trees
Know what species
They are—to what greatness
They may rise:
Reaching toward that
Preordained height
Their nature allows
And their fortune hallows.
Increasing, sowing
Seedpods and catkins
That a future forest
Of individualists
Will be assured.
In this mulligan world
Such family strictness
And integrity is
Profoundly moving;

More than other beings
An artist should keep
The pathway open
To his inward life,
To that native self
That must daily be fed,
Pondered and watered
If what might be
Is to turn—by grace, by craft—into poetry.

For Katherine Anne Porter

MAY 15TH, 1965

Madam, a siege
    Of heron
        Salutes you!

A spring of teal
    Flies criss-cross
        Through golden

Runnels of air, to say
    Luck, good omens!
        While a muster of peacock

Shows all-out
    Best wishes, a flight
        Of doves sends love;

A murmuration of starlings
    Builds up its iridescent
        Agreement

In trees, over fields; and then
    A watch of nightingales
        Flies in to do honor,—

And flies in through this fine
    Evening, to grace what all feel:
        An exaltation of larks!

A Short Way by Air

Between now and the moment when you touch
Down at the end of your trip, so much
Will happen. Before you lies
A legendary fairground, whose size
Measures the days ahead; a carrousel
Swings round and round, its bright mounts fall
And rise as did our breathing—carrying
The scenes and persons of your travelling,
Each for a moment outlined legibly
Against a mulberry sky
That fades to dawn or ripens into night.
                              The light
Brushes tower after tower, or swaying
Into the past a palace topples, as round again
The equestrian hours throng. . . . I look far out
Over what lies before me—a prospect
Of absence, whose extent I shall
Count over; the everyday is genial
Enough, but there was never such
Warmth, for me, as when we are in touch.

Ode to Poseidon

LINES ON A GRECIAN URN RECENTLY ACQUIRED
BY THE WILLIAMS COLLEGE MUSEUM OF ART

Well, hail, Poseidon! Old mariner who was caught
Between brothers—Zeus and Hades—but
    There you are, bent
    On sinking your new trident
Into the vitals of poor Polybotes,
Who rears back upon space as if a cot
    Waited; only his shield,
    A lion, will not yield,
But, twitching its black tear-drop tail,
Glares out at us; Poseidon, hail!

On the vase's other side live three students
Dancing home, exams over, brains spent;
    Life in their heels, they clown
    The cobbled road on down
To celebrate. The central boy knows
What it is to want to *dance*, he fools and shows
    Them who is actor, they
    Are end men; so they play,
Lifting imagined wine in wassail
The students shout: Poseidon, hail!

One wed Poseidon from whom Pegasus
Sprang; no mean feat; many of us
    Know that most able horse,
    Whose love ran with the muse,
Could braid by the very rhythm of his hooves
The formal circlet this vase wears and weaves. . . .
    As to a theatre-in-the-round,
    To lives, music, sound,
How well this winejar brings us in!
Oh, navigator, hail! Poseidon!

PART II   *Vermont Poems—A Cycle*

Moths in Winter

The sun,
Pied-piper this winter day,
Slants warmth in,

And up their glass-
Sheer barrier a moth
Flotilla sculls,

Tissue-paper-
Thin, shell-wings open,
As if there were

A life of days
Ahead; they sway there
Upon black ice,

While night deepens.
Colorless dancers, they long for
The shimmering neon

Inside, like divas
Drawing their wing-capes
Around them, as

Palmed against winter,
White magnets on that darkness
Of death, they falter.

Cold is the dancer.

The Snow Hole

This morning early we came straight out of the house,
Over the saddle of the nearest ridge
To catch up with a logging-road,
Then off, cross-country on our own,
On to the edge of landscape
To visit the sun.

We look ahead—ash and pine
Bristle over their summit.
The air is colder. As we climb
The sun bobs and treads ether.
Across the valley, down their great otter's slide,
Utility poles are pegged one after one.

          Then at the top,
Our heads against the sky,
We see what folk tale promised:—a cleft, a seam
Of purple whiteness nailed to earth,
Sealed off from light
By barricades of stone: a deaf white shaft.
This snow will never melt. Chilled through
By now, we touch the world.

The Cicisbeae

Mincing on slippered feet,
Decked out in sad mandarin-pale faces,
A pride of women flock to The Broad Motel
To sing a song of sixpence.

Tripping on bound feet,
Quilted into identical wrappers, they
Take turn and turnabout through the bedroom turnstyle
With State Senators, with expenses.

Mouths, bellies, feet
Clutch in spasm, let go, get up, go;
Some pocket money, all drink: this is the Social
Hour; the Chair presents

His platform:—each to sing her favorite
Ditty before he'll let her leave: *Careless
Love, Only the Lonely, A Small
Hotel* . . . "Next week, O.K.? Sure, tax exempt!"

Radar and Unmarked Cars

Love at our age
    Goes far:—
        Desires:
            Unmarked cars:

Weave their way through
    The skein
        Of traffic,
            Then again. . . .

Radar:
    A sensitive
        Alignment:
            Two who love:

Gentle
    The hand upon
        The wheel:
            Communication.

To travel
    This highway
        Is intricate
            We may

Not pass
    Those unmarked cars
        Always, but our
            Radar

Will hold us true:
    We need
        Love
            At a constant speed.

Town Meeting Tuesday

Our roadside trees seem to be gathering
Their forces; just the last few days they've changed
From hibernation to life—can they feel spring
A month ahead of time? Is their sap flowing

Already? Something processional in their bearing,
A flexing of boughs, so grey and strict all winter,
An implied fullness sign this lane of tree
On tree's covenant with spring—rose, purple, sepia.

The Lonely Box

Set it beside that gray
Proportion, a meeting-house:
Where more men face
Each other than the altar; eyes
Look level. In turn, in this
New England chapel, the clear
Windows are stained by night and day.

Under its gray
Antenna, eyes hitched
To that corrugated T
V cheek, linked
By light, each is alone;
Shuffling humanity, it sorts
Good guys from bad,
Aiming its lens
To tattoo on each brain
Its violence; alone,
We join an alloy world. . . .

Reflection
Reaches the gray arches,
Clean distances where eyes
May look across the way
And size up good and evil.

An Epithalamium

FOR P. & F. P.

These perfect days
Of the summer solstice
Hang like greening fruit in the air;
It is a magic time, and there
Are harmonies
In view; we praise

Lives in unison,
That ring out strong;
As this full time of year hovers,
Turning, so does your sounding love
Turn toward a long
Green life, with benison.

A Rune for C.

Luck? I am upset. My dog is ill.
I am now in that grey shuttling trains go in for;
The sky clouds, it is hard to believe dawn will

Ever show up.—I look for omens:
Not birds broken, not Fords lashed around trees,
But some item showing that fate is open. . . .

Sometimes, far far down in the magical past
Of us all, in something that stutters, something that rises,
There is an intimation of luck just

Swinging over our way: a cat's paw loose
In the bannisters; a long train-run, and then,
Square and oil-shambled, blue between elms, the caboose!

Looking Up at Leaves

No one need feel alone looking up at leaves.
There are such depths to them, withdrawal, welcome,
A fragile tumult on the way to sky.
This great trunk holds apart two hemispheres
We lie between. . . . Like water lilies
Leaves fall, rise, waver, echoing
On their blue pool, whispering under the sun;
While in this shade, under our hands the brown
Tough roots seek down, lily roots searching
Down through their pool of earth to an equal depth.
Constant as water lilies we lie still,
Our breathing like the lapping of pond water,
Balanced between reflection and reflection.

Headlong

Setting off home, I ran over a woodchuck.
He lunged out—no sleight-of-wheel could have missed
His pepper-and-salt wedge head; a young fellow,
For whom the graveled roadside provided
A grainy banquet. Well, he was quite dead
When I backed up to see what I had done.

This is an old story. Only wisdom
Can read the plane geometry of this tale:
He crossing from one side of the road to the other
For nutriment. I moving out from one
Revolving crystal stage toward another,
Along a gravel road shored up by sky
Through that soft summer afternoon; just then
This headlong meeting stopped us: I ran
A gauntlet of chill air the long way home.

The Hourglass

Again and again I come
To a green place, where elm,
Maple and beech flourish,
Where summer builds its own
Attic; I walk alone
Down this conundrum road
Thinking of you, to fall—
As through an hourglass—
Where all I am dissolves
And flows toward. . . .

                     Yet
Thinking of love, I plunge
Back into mystery:
Who am I . . . ? I'm one
Indivisible grain,
Sentient now, though not
To be for long. . . . I am
Because I know I love?
The glass revolves. I am.

Through this paired hourglass
I journey, heels over head,
Identity—love—
One road, a roof of trees,
Myself a saltimbanque
Between realities.

Running into Edgar Bellemare

In my fool seigneurial car
I came storming through dust, whirling around the corner:
Bang into skidding-distance of skidding
Bellemare, his unfledged wife, four sorry
Towheaded chicks under five, in their Hupmobile.

It amounted to little more than *Plunk:*
Their egg-shell auto crumpled. We sat on
And stared at this odd joining;
And then, unspanning, took off again
About our business. The big car pawed the road
Less mettlesomely. The Bellemares
Went on back down to find a spare fender
At Hawkes' junkyard; all of them to huddle—
Sheltered by that fender—a little longer,
Armored for life by a breastplate frailer than wishbone.

A Few Days Ago

That dark adventure was a tree,
A beldame spruce, inside whose trunk
The sap flowed secretly

Threaded to what had gone before;
Each mood or prospect had kinship
Through that slim corridor

From tap-root to leaf filament.
I found myself enclosed within
The experience. It lent

Its temper to those days, until
It was all over.—Relieved,
I moved again at will

Without that darkness ruling me,
Nor swept along in the winey sap
Of that wind-shaken tree.

What will follow? Things come upon
Us unexpectedly. I wonder
What image or condition

Will bind my next fortnight together:
The stately rising of an elm
Or sullen golden straw?

On Falling Asleep in a Mountain Cabin

We climbed together up to our mountain cabin,
Into a wooden room,
To live with the squirrels for one night.
Crickets clack-clacked, a mouse skittered;
Even the trees had disappeared, leaning to rest
On the deserted dark.

We too lay down. . . .
Under the single bulb the shadows rocked,
Our breath ballooned in the cold;
The icebox whirred: an outboard motor
Propelled us on, nearer the shoals of sleep.

One son dropped off, his faun's eyes
Leafy in the wavering light, the other lay
Brooding over a book; night lobbed
A dog's bark two miles up.
Our pine cabin was cool with the next season.
A short portage from home, we were deep in fall;
Summer, below, clear as a millpond lay—
That green expanse where we had dreamed all day.

Landscape, Deer Season

Snorting his pleasure in the dying sun,
The buck surveys his commodious estate,
Not sighting the red nostrils of the gun
Until too late.

He is alone. His body holds stock-still,
Then like a monument it falls to earth;
While the blood-red target-sun, over our hill,
Topples to death.

Late November Window

A light turns on among the trees, it glows
Through a forest of filetted bones; a lamp
Shimmers just over the carapace of the hill;
Then fades, blurs; waxes, glows.

Stars are not bright enough
To warn if the clouds reel
Awash in the firmament,
Or what ne'er-do-well in the dead
Of night is out hunting the living.

Under the phantasmagoria of sky
Our earth lies black, secret; only that brilliance
Waiting to dazzle a stag, to flash
Death in his eyes.—Oh, but that light
Has cleared our arc of trees; is it then simply
The moon out jacking deer; and fear and I?

The Dressmaker's Dummy as Scarecrow

On the hillside's upper garden a dressmaker's dummy
Is set among carrot and cress.
No longer can she swivel
In rooms that faces have panelled, eyeballs lit,
Informing stuff with her articulate line;
For an outside world she now stands sentinel
Against the crows, the shy
Foraging rodents who patter
By crisscross paths nearer by.

There is at times a blindspot in our view
When one sees nothing, is nothing, cannot see
How one has drifted here;
                    At that breaking-point, one is out of place
As a dressmaker's dummy left there under the sky:
Outside, she is her livery, but changed,
Apart, surrounded by garden; the fern
At the end of perspective
Reaches now to her shoulder;
The moles are wiser and the crows are older;
She may, or she may not, outlast the winter—
The spring may find her still, and grow towards her.

A Night Picture of Pownal

FOR JFK

Thanks to the moon,
Branches of our trees are coral
Fans, cast on the lanky snow
Which, crusted though,

Takes impressions
As Matthew Brady's eye received
The desperation of Civil War;
He was its retina

And watched history
Rise and set. Above its kilt
Of steel-blue air the moon turns,
A circle leans

To stare down fissures
Of space to that black forest set
Like matchsticks on the white hillside;
All sound has died.

Our apple tree
Prints its own photograph, its strong
Branches espaliered on the snow
Fading, will not go

From our minds, the clean
Etching of dark on white, each detail
Tuned to the whole; in its precision
Enduring as bone.

What we have seen
Has become history; tragedy
Marks its design upon the brain-
We are stained by its stain.

Leaning into Light

Our hibiscus, larch,
    Marjoram, cork tree,
        Dandelion seek
            Light—
    A dull day
Has them listless, olive-
Green, no sap running,

As I in a bad
    Time am in shadow,
        Uncertain. But then
            Light,
      Like a prophet,
  Calling them forth
To grow in the sun's great

Eye—as wistaria
    Climbs toward day—
        They revive; I have known
            Light
      Too, a presence
  One turns round to face,
Leans into and joins.

A NOTE ABOUT THE AUTHOR

BARBARA HOWES was born and brought up in Boston, and she attended Bennington College. From 1943 to 1947 she edited the literary quarterly Chimera *in New York, and her first book of poetry,* The Undersea Farmer, *was published in 1948. Five years later* In the Cold Country *followed, and in 1959 came* Light and Dark. *The present collection, much of which has appeared in* The New Yorker, Poetry, The New Republic, Encounter, The Virginia Quarterly Review, *and other magazines, is Barbara Howes's fourth volume of poetry. She has also edited two notable collections of short stories:* 23 Modern Stories *and* From the Green Antilles: Writings of the Caribbean. *In 1955 she received a Guggenheim Fellowship and in 1958 a Brandeis University Creative Arts Poetry Grant. After spending four years in Italy and some time in various islands of the West Indies, she now lives with her family in North Pownal, Vermont.*

A NOTE ON THE TYPE

This book is set in Monotype Bell, a copy of the English Monotype face of the same name. The Englishman John Bell (1745–1831) was responsible for the original cutting of this design. The vocations of Bell were many—among a few might be mentioned bookseller, printer, publisher, type-founder, and journalist. His types were considerably influenced by the delicacy and beauty of the French copper-plate engravers. Monotype Bell might also be classified as a delicate and refined rendering of Scotch Roman.

The book was designed by Betty Anderson and was composed, printed, and bound by Kingsport Press, Inc., Kingsport, Tennessee.